I0449263

Emotional Intelligence

The Real Journey of Becoming as the Master of your Mind to Acquire Social Skills, Mindfulness, Improved Interpersonal Skills & Master Your Questions of Leadership Skills & Self Confidence

By:

John McAndrew

Published by 42 Enterprises Publishing,
All Rights Reserved,
Copyright 2016, Cincinnati, Ohio

Table of Contents

Introduction

Intelligence is one of the most importanttraits that enables a person to succeed in life. Regular intelligence is very important to success but emotional intelligence is the skill that one needs in order to be able to relate well with other people. This is the skill that willhelp you achieve your goals in life. Emotional intelligence is therefore as important as the regularintelligence, which is why many employers are testing the emotional intelligence of prospective employees before allocating positions tothem.

Emotionalintelligencecovers a large area in the life of a humanbeing. It is theskill that helps you to know your actionsand feelings better and also to understand how these affect the peoplethat you meet every day.

People with well-developed emotional intelligence are able to value other people more and this is shown through their willingness to listen and understand their needs and wants and to identify with them in different levels.

Emotional intelligence is necessary to attain success in your career as well as your social life. Through it, you have total control of your emotions feelings and actions and you can always relate well with other people in your life.

This book covers everything that you need in order to develop your emotional intelligence to ensure that you are in a better position to succeed in life as a human being and as a professional. All the important aspects of emotional intelligence have been explained in detail.

Chapter 1:
Emotional Intelligence Basics

There are smart people around us, who always have something good to say in all situations, and they know how to say it. These are the same people who will listen to you until you finish what you have to say. Theseare the people who will not offend you in any way, because they know how to say everything, even the ugly truth. They are usually verycaring and considerate and they willmake you feel better even if theywill not offer a solution to the issue that you are facing.

These are people who are able to manage their emotions. Theyremain relaxed even when the situation is depressing. They face their problems calmly in order to find a solution without getting emotional about it.

They are also very good in decision making. Theywill know when to trust their intuition in order to know if the solution they want to go for is the right one ornot. They do not perceive themselves as perfect; they always face the reality and will take criticism positively. They will also take advantage of the criticism in order to better their performance.

Theseare emotionally intelligence people. They have taken time to learn about themselves in order to know what is right and wrong for them. From that, they are able to know the emotional needs of other people in order to make them feel better even in stressful situations.

What is Emotional Intelligence?

Every person has their own personality, needs and wants. Everyone has their own way of expressing their emotions. All these require a smart way of navigating through them especially if you want to appear smart and successful in life and this is the importance of emotional intelligence.

Emotional intelligence is hence defined as the ability for one to recognize their emotions, to understand what other people are saying to them and to realize how their emotions are affecting other people around them. It also entails how you perceive other people and if you understand their feelings as this is what helps you form lasting and healthy relationships with them.

For what good is emotional intelligence?

Emotional intelligence is very important. It is highly considered whenever one is looking for a job or a promotion today because it leads to professional success. Organizations are using emotional intelligence as a measure of how smart one is before they are given a good position because this measures how well you will perform and relate with other people working in the organization.

People who are emotionally intelligent are viewed as more successful than the others in everything that they do. This is because these are the people that everyone wants to work and hang around with. These people make other people feel good, therefore when they seek help, they get it very fast. They relate very well with other people, therefore in case they are looking for support, they are highly likely to get it.

Elements that define emotional intelligence

These are the characteristics of emotionally intelligent people:

a) Self-awareness

People with emotional intelligence are so much aware of themselves. They know what upsets them and what makes them happy, and they have total control of their emotions. They do not allow their emotions to overrule them. They have great trust in their instincts, and their emotions do not get out of control, both of which gives them confidence to make decisions.

People who are self-aware are able to look at them honestly to evaluate their strengths and weaknesses in order to know the areas that need improvement in their lives so as to perform better. This is a very important characteristic and it forms an integral part of emotional intelligence.

b) Empathy

This is another one of the mostimportant elements of emotional intelligence and it entails one's ability to understand theneeds, wants, emotions and views of other people. These are thepeople who will understand the feelings of other people easily even before the people communicate their feelingsand needs to them. They play attention when other people are talking in order to understand what they are saying deeply. Thesepeople are excellent in relationships because they donot judge or stereotype other people. They will be open and honest with the people they are in relationships with.

c) Motivation

People with good emotional intelligence are highly motivated. They do not focus so much on short-term results but on long term success. These are the kinds of people who will focus on productivity and they will take a challenge just to prove to themselves how smart they are. As a result, these people are very effective.

d) Self-regulation

This entails one's ability to control their impulses and emotions. Many people fail terribly in life because they are unable to control their impulsive and careless behavior. With emotional intelligence, you will not make any impulsive or careless decision or get too angry easily, or even jealous. These are the kinds of people who think about something before they get involved in it. Self-regulation is good because it leads to thoughtfulness, integrity, ability to say no and also ability to change when situations call for it.

e) Social skills

People with high emotional intelligence are very good in talking and getting along with other people. They fit very well in groups, and they are good team players. They do not work to improve themselves first, but on holding others and supporting them in order to attain success together. These are the people who are happy when they see others shine and they would do anything to help other people succeed. They are able to settle disputes and very good in communication, making them the best people to get into relationships with.

They are able to overcome their social anxiety in order to connect effectively to other people.

These are the characteristics that makes people with emotional intelligence successful in life especially in their careers. This is because emotional intelligence revolves around being able to manage people and relationships. Leaders for instance are required to have excellent emotionalintelligence. This is thus an important skill to master for anyone that wants to be a leader someday.

Chapter 2:
Acquisition of Social Skills

Human beings have been created with the ability to socialize with others and this is the way through which they are able to communicate their thoughts, feelings and pass messages to one another. What you say to other people is measured by the way you verbally say it and also in the way that you say it, which is through the tone of your voice, the volume of your speech and in the kinds of words you choose. The body language, gestures and all the other non-verbal communication methods also matter so much during communication.

Unfortunately, some people communicate better than the others and this is what has necessitated the need for investigations into the nature and the purpose of relational interaction in order to evaluate the real cause of this.

People develop social skills differently and this entails being aware of how you communicate with other people. And the types of messages that you send to other people. A person who has developed social skills is also able to know how he can improve his communication in order to communicate more efficiently and effectively to all the people.

Advantages of developing social skills

1. Better and more relations

    Social skills helps you to identify well with other people and this is what promotes relationships. A person who relates well with other people is able to make more friends in the end. Social skills makes a person more charismatic, which is a trait that attracts other people to you. You are able to attract other people as you are attracted to them and this is what makes it easy for you to form lasting relations.

What people need to know is that it is hard to go far in this life without strong and meaningful interpersonal relationships. Relationships are for instance what will get you a good job, get you new friends and also get you a promotion.

Social skills also increase your happiness and enhances satisfaction in life. You are better able to look at life in apositive way and this is what curtails stress and feelings follow self-esteem.

2. Efficiency

People who are able to communicate well with others are able to know the right people to relate with and those who are not. You can easily know the viewpoints and interests of other people and this is what tells you how you will relate with those people. Efficiency comes about when you are able to attend a meeting with all kinds of people because you know what their view about life is and how they perceive things that affect all of you. A person with great communication skills is also able to fit in any setting because he can effectively communicate with all kinds of people, irrespective of their perceptions and views.

3. Enhanced communication

Social skills helps you relate well with other people and this is what enables you to work with other people even in large groups, and in the end, your communication skills are enhanced. There is no way you will have social skills without being able to communicate well, because this is what brings you closer to other people. Better communication skills are what helps you to communicate your thoughts and ideas to other people,

4. Better career predictions

Careers are very important today and they are chosen depending on your level of social skills. This is because most of the important positions in many organizations and companies entail spending time with other employees, bosses, the media and clients, that is why your social skills can be used to determine the right jobs to apply for. Many jobs requires one to work with other people. There is no single time that you will be required to work all alone in an office, which is why employers are continually looking for good social skills whenever they are recruiting. You need good social skills to be able to influence others to work better and also to work with other people in a team.

5. Happiness and satisfaction

Social skills helps you to get along with other people and this opens up paths of relating well with other people and doors of career success, which brings happiness and satisfaction in life. Imagine what confidence to air your opinion and to answer questions in a conference can bring? You can get a good job proposition without even presenting your application letter. A smile can bring a great friend who can help you in so many ways in life.

How can you improve your social skills?

Good social skills are paramount for people who want to live a healthy, happy and a fun life. Good social skills leads to good mental health. That is why it is important to learn how you can improve your social skills. This is the only way you will be confident, charming and able to form healthy and lasting relationships. Human beings are able to improve on their social skills through looking back to how they have behaved in the past and also through practice. Here are some of the things that you can do in order to improve your social skills to be able to communicate and relate well with other people:

✓ Improving your verbal communication

To do this, you have to be aware of the volume and tone of your voice whenever you are communicating. Avoid being too loudly or even too soft when you are speaking. You should be audible and also able to convey confidence and not to seem aggressive.

Master the effective way of starting a conversation. If you are in the midst of other people, start talking about generalthings for instance about the weather, a current event or generally making an observation about something that concernsevery one of you.

Look for a way to extend a conversation. If you are meeting up with a new person, it is not easy to know what to say to them. Once you start with general topics, you should find a way to bring some personal issues that are not too intimate, which the other person will find interesting. This way, you will be able to converse for a little longer. This does not mean that you dominate the conversation though; you should know that a conversation is between two people or among many people, therefore you should avoid saying too much, the same way you should be avoiding saying too little.

Do not get involved with inciting talk. A person that you do not know so well is not easy to converse with because you do not know their views about so many things. You should therefore stick to subjects that are comfortable and not too personal. You may speak about politics for instance but not personal views about a certain candidate.

Once the conversation is over, end it courteously. Many people upset others without knowing it when they cut short their conversation and end it abruptly. This is not what to do for someone who wants to improve their social skills. You have to be polite and announce that you have to leave, and apologizefor ending it too soon. Then you can thank them for their time.

✓ Improving your nonverbal communication

Like I mentioned earlier, your nonverbal communication is as important as the verbal communication when you are passing a message to another person. You have to improve on it too when you are working on your socials kills. To do this:

Evaluate your body language as this is what the other person pays attention to, more than the verbal message. You have to be aware of the kinds of messages you pass along through your body posture, your facial expressions, and your eyes among other significant body parts.

Always meet people with a smile as it is the only way to open up to other people to talk to you. Taking time to create a rapport makes people feel at ease around you.

Practice on maintaining eye contact in all your conversations with other people, because it urges them to continue talking to them. You are also able to understand people better when you pay attention to what they are saying and how they are saying it.

✓ Practice socializing with people

You have to start somewhere, which is why this is an important stage in improving your socialskills. Try to converse with people that are not familiar with you for instance, even for a few minutes. You can visit places where you are likely to meet new faces, then strike a conversation with one person or two.

Whenever you are looking for a person to talk to, try to pick someone that is less busy and one that looks easy to talk to. Evaluate the results and do it again if you are getting good results from this. This should boost your esteem for people with a low self-esteem.

Chapter 3:
Interpersonal Skills

Interpersonal skills are the skills that we use in order to interact with other people effectively. In a job setting for instance, interpersonal skillshelpsone to relate well with their colleagues at the same time ensuring that they are working as effective as they should. Interpersonal skills need to be well developed because they lead to success not just personal success but professional success as well.

Employersthese days are hiring employees with strong interpersonal skills because these are thekinds of people who will work very wellwith others in a team and at the same time be able to maintain a good relationship with their colleagues, the customers and also the clients.

People with developed interpersonal skills are usually calm, confident, optimistic and also charismatic, which are some of the traits that attract others to form good relationships.

Interpersonal skills comprise of the following skills:

- Verbal communication skills, which involves what you say and how you say it

- Nonverbal communication skills which entail how you communicate without words.

- Problem solving skills which includes the ability for one to work with others to identify a problem, define it and then work together to solve the problem

- Listening skills which includes how you interpret the verbal and nonverbal communication that is directed to you by others.

- Decision making skills which entails exploring and examining choices that will help you make comprehensive decisions

- Negotiation skills which includes how well you work with other people in order to find a solution that is agreeable to allthe parties

- Assertive skills which helps one to communicate their beliefs, values, ideas, needs, opinions and their wants without restrictions

Every human being has been developing their interpersonal skills ever since they were born. This is usually subconsciously because these are skills that come naturally to us. However, there are times you take them for granted, for instance the way that you talk to another person, and this affects the kind of relationship you have with that person. It is important to know that it takes less effort to develop interpersonal skills in order to improve so many aspects of our lives.

How to improve and develop one's interpersonal skills

a) Learn to listen to other people. You should pay attention to both the verbal and the nonverbal communication in order to understand what they are saying.

b) Show some empathy. This entails trying to see things in other people's perspective. It is important to know that we all cannot have the same opinion about things and life. Trying to empathize helps us to learn something new from other people and this can help us in decision making and problem solving.

c) Pick your words carefully despite the situation. The words that you use when talking to other people matter a lot. People can misunderstand you or even confuse what you are saying through the words that you use. Ensure that you are absolutely clear and always seek feedback so as to be sure that your message has been understood well.

d) Always stay optimistic and cheerful. People are attracted to people who are positive minded. Besides, it is the only way you will be able to communicate well with other people, because you can see something good in all of them.

e) Learn to be assertive. This means being confident about yourself. This is achieved through not being too aggressive nor too passive. You should be able to express your feelings and communicate your beliefs, needs and wants freely without holding back. This should always be done in a way that other people can understand. If you want to negotiate successfully with other people, you really have to be self-assertive.

f) Find out why communication fails. You should not always expect to communicate effectively. There are at times when the communication fails due to the various barriers to effective communication. Learning why communication fails can help you device ways through which you can overcome communication barriers that affect your communication.

g) Learn to work in groups. It is impossible to live all alone in this world. We always find ourselves in group situations, both socially and professionally, therefore learning how to work in group is an important skill that can impact on your interpersonal skills. Start by understanding the different types of groups you are in, then learn how to work in those groups.

h) Relax in all situations. There is no way you will speak clearly and communicate effectively when you are nervous, that is why you should stay relaxed. Try to calm down before you start communicating because everyone will see how tense you are and they will not pay much attention to what you are saying. When you are relaxed, try to maintain an eye contact and keep smiling to feel at ease among other people.

i) Seek for clarity. This is the only way you will understand what other people are saying well. You should show interest when someone else is talking to you and ask questions in between in order to understand better. In case of a misunderstanding, ensue that you clarify it with the other person.

j) Understand and manage stress. Stress affects people from all walks of life. It is important to learn how to recognize stress and also to manage it. It is also more important to learn how you can reduce the stress that affects you and also one that affects other people. Stress may not be so much but it is good to know that it can affect the way that you communicate with other people.

Chapter 4:
Self Confidence

Self-confidence is what comes after you assure yourself about your ability, personal judgment, and power, among others. Unfortunately, not all people have self-confidence, even the most known leaders. People who have self-confidence are able to inspire others to have confidence in themselves.

Self-confidence is always not static; it is something that will take some effort to maintain especially when things are not going according to plan. You have to learn to be confidence about yourself, then practice the skill and later on master it, just like everyone else that is important. Mastering self-confidence is the most important bit because it changes everything about your life.

How to effectively promote self confidence

i) Show it through your body language: self-confidence has to be demonstrated through your body language. You need to act self- reassured, otherwise people will see how insecure you are about yourself. You have to be confident whenever you are meeting people so that they can see how ready and able you are to take charge of the situation. This is what makes you feel in total control over the situation and other people will start believing in your ability.

For self-confidence, you have to hold your head high and you have to maintain a straight posture whenever you are speaking to other people. Be firm when you are speaking with people, and even in your handshake.

ii) Always act and think positively: a positive mind will always bring forth positive results, therefore get rid of the negative self-talk and go for a positive feeling and thoughts that will push you to do what you set your mind to do. Even when you have a great responsibility ahead, a positive thought is what makes it easy to handle. This is what boost your confidence, and you start feeling able to do just about anything.

A positive thought comes when you feel happy, therefore try to smile in all situations. Also, surround yourself with people who are happy and positive minded. They will boost your confidence in believing that you can do everything and face any situation that comes your way.

Positivity has to be insisted upon, because when things start going against your expectations, you may start doubting your ability. To overcome this, keep a journal of the things that you have achieved in the past. Your past accomplishments will make you see how capable you are.

iii) Dress well: you have to look great to feel great, and this is where the physical look comes in. For this to happen, you have to choose your clothes and accessories well, clothes that fit you well and those that match the situation and event.

People need to learn to dress their personalities, as this is what will sell you out to other people. Do not try to overdress as people will focus on what you are wearing other than what you are saying to them. You have to consider the people you are meeting with as well when you are dressing in order to pass the right message across to them through your dressing.

iv) Speak with a lot of confidence: you have to command confidence to feel confident about yourself and this is what makes you a great speaker. Choose to speak assertively and ensure that you are not sounding aggressive in any way. When people start accepting you, your self-esteem will be boosted and they will start trusting what you are telling them, because you already feel confident about it.

v) Set and meet small goals before going to the next ones: one killer of self-confidence is unrealistic goals, because they tell you how incapable you are, since you will not meet them in the end. If you are working on your self-confidence, start with smaller and achievable goals and increase on them as you go on. Setting high and unrealistic goals will discourage you and make you feel as if you are incapable of doing something. In as much as it helps to aim high, you should set goals which you are sure to achieve as this is what boosts your confidence and you can work even harder in order to achieve more.

vi) Do not delay taking action: confidence is not just in how you feel but how you act too. A lot of people are scared of starting something and it can take them more time than it should because it took them a longer time to get started. When you are confident about yourself, you should be able to start something right away. If therefore you are still learning how to develop your self-confidence, teach yourself to act immediately, when it is required. If for instance you are looking for people to network with, do not take time to think about it. Approach the people you feel will be beneficial to you.

vii) Increase your competence: this is one of the things that makes a person feel more confident about themselves. People who are smart are more confident in themselves and they feel free to air their views in meetings and social gatherings. You have to be more competent to feel more competent and this is through pursuit of knowledge. You have to study more and practice more to increase your competence. You do not have to do so much at once; start small and get better with time. This will make you feel at ease when you are in the midst of people with high competencies, just like you.

Chapter 5:
Leadership Skills

Leadership responsibilities and roles are always all around us, not just in our places of work. These are skills you can easily apply in any life situation mainly in places where you are required to take the lead. You can apply these skills socially, professionally, among your friends or even at home. It is easy to spot a leader because of their integrity and people are always willing to follow them.

Contrary to what many people say, leadership skills cannot be trained. Many successful leaders all over the world do not have any formal training on leadership. For these people, leadership skills come from the mind. What makes them successful is their traits and their personalities.

One thing that people need to know is that leaders are different; you will not find leaders who are exactly the same. Every leader has their own leadership style which they use in order to effectively lead their groups.

A lot is involved in leadership and this is for instance:

- Your ability to direct, organize, persuade and to motivate other people
- Taking the initiative in everything that needs to be done
- Taking responsibility of the actions and the direction that your team takes
- Being able to set objectives and goals
- Being able to accept responsibility in case of a mistake or a wrong decision

- Persevering when things get rough

- Remaining positive even in case of a frustration or a failure

- Flexibility and ability to change as per changing situations

There are people with great leadership skills and these are easily voted in by other people to be their leaders. Emotional intelligence requires one to polish up their leadership skills in order to shine when working with other people.

How to develop your leadership skills

✓ Take the initiative to act as a leader in every opportunity that presents itself. This is the only way you will show yourself as a leader even before other people vote you in as one. Many employers love people who take the lead and this is something that can earn you a good reward and favor in the organization. You do not have to wait for other people to see the leader in you when you can show them how great a leader you can be.

✓ Take charge of your own objectives. Being able to set objectives is a great skill in leadership. You should not only set great objectives but also be able to take responsibility of those objectives. You need to be able to know which objectives should be prioritized and which ones should come last.

✓ Try to do more than you have been asked. You do not have to stick to your job description.A good leader will go an extra mile just to show how passionate they are in whatever they are doing. As an aspiring leader, you should do things that will get you noticed easily.

✓ Always show your ability to do things however difficult they might seem. You need to have an attitude of ability too, even when other people are almost losing hope. This is what will enable you to try to solve issues other than passing them to other people. Keep trying and see how much you can do.

✓ Keep learning new skills that will helpyou improve the way you work. Your abilities are the onesthat will sell you out to the people you should be leading. You should therefore be willing to acquire more skills that will make you a better leader for the people to recognize you.

✓ Always be enthusiastic in whatever that you do. People love a person who will work cheerfully even when they are not rewarded for it. This is what will get you great rewards such as promotions in your organization.

✓ Constantly think of ways through which you can improve situations wherever you are and communicate your feelings to other people. You should not be contented with what is already available. You should propose improvements to the way things have always been done with a hope of making things better.

✓ In case of any problems, mistakes and failures, you should be able to accept them without putting a blame on someone else or something. A good leader should always expect problems, therefore you should know what you will do once a problem comes up in order to solve it once and for good.

Things that will make you a charismatic leader

- ❖ A good eye contact will always set you apart from other leaders

- ❖ Show and tell people how much they matter and how much you enjoy being with them.

- ❖ You should be able to develop a genuine smile

- ❖ Always portray an open posture to show other people that you are the person they should be dealing with

- ❖ Stay relaxed at all times even when things are not going on well

- ❖ Keep your head straight to show how confident you are

- ❖ Treat all people with kindness and equality however significant or less significant they might be

People skills

All leaders need to have well developed people skills as these arethe skillsthat helpthemlead people better. There is no way youwill be a good leader if there will be no people to lead, which is why this is a very important area for leadership skills.

Every leader need proper skills that willhelp them work well with other people. Youshould be abletowork one on one with other people as well as in a group. Leaders also need to have good tools that will help them deal with the various situations that they face with the people they lead.

Here are some people skills leaders should have:

- ❖ Delegation skills- this is not an easy skill for many people but if it is done well, it can give everyone in a team a sense of responsibility and a chance for them to become a leader in their own field. Delegations help so much if you want to motivate your team to work better. As a leader, you shouldlearn how to delegate as well as how to complimentyour group when they do well so as to build them.

- ❖ Giving and receiving feedback- this isanother great skill that every leader must have. A leader should be ableto ask for feedback as well as give feedback on any responsibility and task that he givesout to his members. The way you talk to your group may construct or destroy them, therefore you have to be careful with your use of words

Chapter 6:
Relationships

Relationships are very important to human beings. Everyone is involved in a relationship of some kind. Relationships are usually built on love. There are different types of relationships that people get involved in and these are:

o   Family relations

o   Friendship relations

o   Sexual relations

Human beings are social by nature. Everyone enjoys a situation wherethey are accepted and understood and this onlyhappensin relationships. The feeling of being loved and a chance to love is also present in relationships. This is why people that we are in arelationship with are veryimportant to us. You seem to love yourfamily, friends and yoursexual partner more thananyone else in thislife.

People are constantly seeking ways to better their relationships because they have slowly learned that relationships are much better than anything else, including career success. Howgreat would it be if you had the same kind of relationship you had with your significant other in the beginning? How great would it be to feel more appreciated and understood by your friends? How great would it be if you were the one who was admired and accepted as you are by your family?

All this is what should motivate you to try to build better relationships with the people around you. Here are some things you can do:

Listen and aim for understanding

The problem is that people in relationships are usually too busy with their own thoughts to listen for them to understand what the other person issaying. Everyone is engrossed with their own ideas and the desire to outshine the other person to pay attention to what the other person has. It is important to know that other people have great ideas, thoughts and advice too and these can help you a lot, only if you listen. Other people are always talking even when the other person is talking, or patiently waiting for their turn to say something and they do not get what the other person is saying.

For a good relationship to be formed, there should be a good conversation and this requires you to listen to the other person to understand what they are saying. This is the only way you will connect with the other person deeply.

Learn to trust people

So many people have been hurt in the past and others are hurting to date. That is why it seems hard for some people to trust others. Many people have given up on their marriages and other significant relationships because they no longer trust their partners. Even when all this is happening, the truth will always be that every relationship that you will get into will require some form of trust, be it a family relationship, a business relationship, a friendship or even a platonic relationship.

Stop worrying about what other people are doing at a particular time, thinking or even saying when you are not with them. This is what trust is all about. When you lack trust, youwill always want to monitor and to control other people instead of enjoying the kind of relationship you have with them.

Relationships are supposed to be enjoyed not to stress you because without trust, you are always looking for clues that the other person is hurting you.

Be open about what you want in a relationship

People in relationships are always expecting something from their partners and when they do not get it, they get so disappointed. These expectations are the ones that ruin a once great relationship. When you expect something from people without telling them about it, you always end up getting hurt and feeling letdown. The problem is that you do not tell other people what you want from them, then you end up blaming them when they fail to read your mind.

For a good relationship to thrive, you have to be honest about it. You should always feel free to express what you want in order to give the other person a chance to give it to you.

Give more than you receive

Human beings are very selfish by nature because they are always looking for a way to gain something especially from other people. Before getting into a relationship, one would think about what is in it for him without thinking of how it can benefit the other person. In a relationship, things have to workdifferently for the relationship to last for a long time. You have to give something of a greater value than what you receive in order for the other person to want to stay with you.

People are always advised to invest inrelationships andthis is what this is all about. You have to make the significantpeople inyour life feel good at all times and this can be done through gifting them, spending quality time with them and giving them your full attention whenever they are around.

Conclusion

Emotional intelligence is therefore a significant skill for many people who want to succeed in different areas of life. Good news is that the skill can be learned and developed. You have to continually work on the skillto ensure that you are doing well in all the areas that I have mentioned above. There are various strategiesthatone can use in order effectively develop their emotional intelligence.

Pay attention to how you react to other people. Are you the judging type of a person whowill pass on judgment even before youunderstand the other person better? Or are you the stereotyping kind of a person? It is good to honesty know how you react to other people so that you will start learning how you can accept them, together with their needs, wants, beliefs and perspectives.

Evaluate your strengths and weaknesses and accept that you are not perfect. A lot of people view themselves as perfectand when theymakea mistake, they beat themselves up, whichmakes it hard forone to learn something new. Always know that there are so many areas where you need improvement in and work hard to learn something new every day. When you are honest about your strengths and weaknesses, you will develop your abilities really fast.

The other strategy you can use in order to develop your emotional intelligence is by examining how you react to stress. People react differently to stressful situations. There are those people who will get upset and others will blame other people. You need to stay calm and in control of every situation regardless of the stress.